A **Literature Kit™** F O R

Where the Wild Things Are

By Maurice Sendak

Written by Mary-Helen Goyetche

GRADES 1 - 2

Classroom Complete Press

P.O. Box 19729
San Diego, CA 92159
Tel: 1-800-663-3609 / Fax: 1-800-663-3608
Email: service@classroomcompletepress.com

www.classroomcompletepress.com

ISBN-13: 978-1-55319-323-4
ISBN-10: 1-55319-323-7

© 2007

Permission to Reproduce

Critical Thinking Skills

Where the Wild Things Are

Skills For Critical Thinking		Chapter Questions					
		Phonics	Word Study	Comprehension	Reading Response	Writing Tasks	Graphic Organizers
LEVEL 1 Knowledge	• Identify Story Elements		✓	✓			✓
	• Recall Details	✓	✓	✓			✓
	• Match			✓			
	• Sequence			✓			
LEVEL 2 Comprehension	• Compare & Contrast			✓			✓
	• Summarize		✓	✓			
	• Recognize Main Idea			✓			✓
	• Describe			✓			
	• Classify		✓	✓			
LEVEL 3 Application	• Plan				✓		
	• Interview					✓	
	• Make Inferences						
LEVEL 4 Analysis	• Draw Conclusions				✓		✓
	• Recognize Cause & Effect				✓	✓	
LEVEL 5 Synthesis	• Predict					✓	✓
	• Design						
	• Create				✓		
	• Imagine Alternatives				✓	✓	
LEVEL 6 Evaluation	• Opinion				✓	✓	✓
	• Make Judgements					✓	

Based on Bloom's Taxonomy

Contents

✔ **6 BONUS** Activity Pages! Additional worksheets for your students
✔ **3 BONUS** Overhead Transparencies! For use with your projection system

FREE!

- Go to our website: **www.classroomcompletepress.com/bonus**
- Enter item CC2104 – Where the Wild Things Are
- Enter pass code CC2104D for Activity Pages. CC2104A for Overheads.

Assessment Rubric

Where the Wild Things Are

Student's Name: _____ Task: _____ Level: _____

	Level 1	Level 2	Level 3	Level 4
Details	Student can give one detail from the story	Student can give two details from the story	Student can give three details from the story	Student can give four or more details from the story
Characters	Student refers to characters using he or she	Student refers to characters using the boy or the girl	Student refers to characters using names	Student refers to all characters using full names and titles
Information	Student gives incorrect information	Student gives mixed up information	Student gives literal information	Student gives correct information
Questions and Answers	Student cannot answer any teacher questions	Student provides some answers to teacher questions	Student provides correct answers to teacher questions	Student provides thoughtful responses to teacher questions

STRENGTHS:

WEAKNESSES:

NEXT STEPS:

Teacher Guide

Our resource has been created for ease of use by both TEACHERS and STUDENTS alike.

Introduction

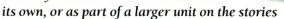

This resource provides ready-to-use information and activities for beginning readers. It can be used in any Language Arts program to strengthen children's **reading, writing** and **thinking skills.** You may wish to use our resource on its own, or as part of a larger unit on the stories of Maurice Sendak, a unit on monsters, adventure stories, etc. It is comprised of interesting and engaging student activities in language, reading comprehension and writing, and can be used effectively for individual, small group or whole class activities.

How Is Our Literature Kit™ Organized?

STUDENT HANDOUTS

Activities in language, reading comprehension and writing (*in the form of reproducible worksheets*) make up the majority of our resource. There are six pages each of PHONICS activities, WORD STUDY activities, COMPREHENSION activities and WRITING tasks. All are either a half-page or full page long. Also provided is a six-page mini-booklet of READING RESPONSE activities. All of these activities contain words and/or phrases from the story which will help the students learn, practice and review important vocabulary words. The writing tasks and reading response mini-book provide opportunities for students to think and write both critically and creatively about the story. It is not expected that all activities will be used, but are provided for variety and flexibility in the unit.

- Also provided are two puzzles, a **word search** and **crossword**. Each of these worksheets can be completed as individual activities or done in pairs.
- Three **Graphic Organizers** are included to help develop students' thinking and writing skills (*see page 6 for suggestions on using the Graphic Organizers*). The **Assessment Rubric** (*page 4*) is a useful tool for evaluating students' responses to many of the

activities in our resource. The **Comprehension Quiz** (*page 46*) can be used for either a follow-up review or assessment at the completion of the unit.

DISCUSSION QUESTIONS

It is a good idea to introduce a new story to students by preparing them for reading. Using a read-aloud approach, you may wish to open a discussion with the **Before You Read** Discussion Questions (*see page 9*) in the Teacher Guide. Then, read the story out loud. As you are reading, use the **As You Read** questions to engage the students in the story. Once you have completed the read-aloud and the students are familiar with the story, follow-up with the **After You Read** questions. You can present the After You Read questions orally for a continued whole group discussion, or write them on the chalkboard and have students discuss possible answers in small groups and then report back to the class.

PICTURE CUES

Our resource contains three main types of pages, each with a different purpose and use. A Picture Cue at the top of each page shows, at a glance, what the page is for.

🍎 **Teacher Guide**
- Information and tools for the teacher

✏️ **Student Handout**
- Reproducible worksheets and activities

☑️ **Easy Marking™ Answer Key**
- Answers for student activities

EASY MARKING™ ANSWER KEY

Marking students' worksheets is fast and easy with our **Answer Key**. Answers are listed in columns – just line up the column with its corresponding worksheet, as shown, and see how every question matches up with its answer!

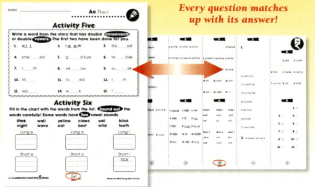

Every question matches up with its answer!

1,2,3
Graphic Organizer Transparencies

The three **Graphic Organizer Transparencies** included in our **Literature Kit™** are especially suited to a study of ***Where the Wild Things Are*** . Below are suggestions for using each organizer in your classroom, or they may be adapted to suit the individual needs of your students. The transparencies can be used on an overhead projector in teacher-led activities, and/or photocopied for use as student worksheets. To evaluate students' responses to any of the organizers, you may wish to use the **Assessment Rubric** (*on page 4*).

DEALING WITH ANGER

This graphic organizer helps students see their problems and their reactions. Have them write down, in the first column, their problems or difficult situations that they have been in. Have them describe how they handled their problems in the second column. In the third column, students write down how they could have handled that situation (or a similar one in future) in a better way. By reflecting on their reactions, maybe next time they will have a more positive or effective response. You can collect the organizers and read one problem a day, having the children brainstorm appropriate behavior and responses.

Found on Page 53.

ME AND MAX

Ask the children, "Do you see yourself in Max?" Most children will connect to, or see themselves in Max in some way. In the first circle, the students are asked to write things that describe them. In the second circle, the students are asked to write things that describe Max. In the space that overlaps, they are to write things that describe both of them. With a partner, have the children share what they have in common with Max. Then, see how as a group they have similar and different qualities and characterisitics with Max.

Found on Page 54.

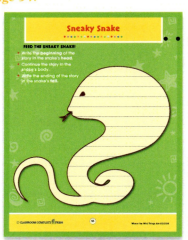

SNEAKY SNAKE

Tell the children that for this activity, they will feed the sneaky snake! They may begin with the head of the snake or its tail. Either way, they are to write the beginning of the story in the snake's head, and the end of the story in the snake's tail. All of the connecting events are to be written in the body of the snake, in the order they happened. The snake is divided into sections to help the children think of the story in its component parts. The snake shape makes this sequencing activity more fun than an ordinary timeline organizer.

Found on Page 55.

Bloom's Taxonomy* for Reading Comprehension

The activities in our resource engage and build the full range of thinking skills that are essential for students' reading comprehension. Based on the six levels of thinking in Bloom's Taxonomy, questions are given that challenge students to not only recall what they have read, but move beyond this to understand the text through higher-order thinking. By using higher-order skills of application, analysis, synthesis and evaluation, students become active readers, drawing more meaning from the text, and applying and extending their learning in more sophisticated ways.

This **Literature Kit**™, therefore, is an effective tool for any Language Arts program. Whether it is used in whole or in part, or adapted to meet individual student needs, this resource provides teachers with the important questions to ask, inspiring students' interest, creativity, and promoting meaningful learning.

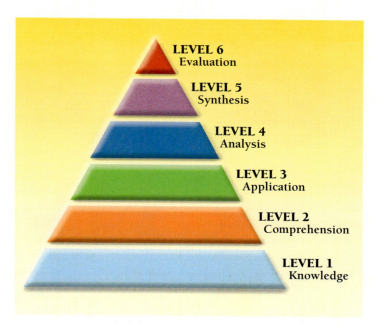

LEVEL 6 — Evaluation
LEVEL 5 — Synthesis
LEVEL 4 — Analysis
LEVEL 3 — Application
LEVEL 2 — Comprehension
LEVEL 1 — Knowledge

**BLOOM'S TAXONOMY:
6 LEVELS OF THINKING**

Bloom's Taxonomy is a widely used tool by educators for classifying learning objectives, and is based on the work of Benjamin Bloom.

Summary of the Story

WHERE THE WILD THINGS ARE

This story is based on a mischievous boy named Max. Dressed up in a wolf suit he chases his dog with a fork and does things he shouldn't. His mom gets upset and calls him a "Wild Thing!" Max retaliates by screaming back to his mom "I'LL EAT YOU UP!" His mom sends him to his room without any supper.

Max doesn't seem to mind, and from within his imagination his room goes from room to forest to ocean with Max inside the little boat where he comes up to the land of "Wild Things". He, of course, is the King of the Wild Things and together they cause quite a rumpus. Max becomes lonely and he smells good things to eat. Wanting to be with someone who loved him best of all, he leaves the land of Wild Things. He comes back to his own room where he finds his supper, still hot, waiting for him.

Vocabulary

Included in our **Literature Kit™** are 20 vocabulary words from **Where the Wild Things Are** in the form of **word cards** (*pages 43 and 44*). The word cards may be used in a variety of hands-on activities. Also included is a page of 10 blank word cards that may be filled in with other words from the story, or words that fit in with a related subject or theme (*page 45*). You may wish to write the words on the cards or have the children add the words themselves.

Here are suggestions for hands-on activities using the word cards. Make photocopies of the cards for each student or for each group of students.

- Have the children classify the words by parts of speech (verbs, nouns, adjectives, etc.).
- Put the cards face down and have students pick 3 or 4 cards; they can write a story inspired by the cards they select (for example, a new adventure about Max).
- Combine and shuffle the vocabulary words with those from another story (perhaps another book by Maurice Sendak, or another story about monsters). Have the children categorize the words by story.
- Have the children use as many word cards as possible to write complete sentences. They will need to write more words on the blank cards (articles, prepositions, etc.)
- Have the children place the words in alphabetical order.
- Have the children work in pairs and each take half of the cards. Without saying the word, one child describes the word on the card, and the other student guesses what the word is.
- Put the cards face down and have students pick up a card and create a word web with it.
- Have the children cut up the words in syllables.

almost	blink	claws	day	eyes
gnashed	hung	mischief	ocean	private
roared	rumpus	still	tamed	terrible
thing	vines	week	wild	year

Suggestions for Further Reading

BOOKS BY MAURICE SENDAK

Mommy?, © 2006

Very Far Away, © 2003

Higglety, Pigglety Pop!: Or There Must Be More to Life, © 1995

In the Night Kitchen, © 1996

Chicken Soup with Rice: A Book of Months, © 1990

Alligators All Around, © 1990

Outside Over There, © 1981

Discussion Questions

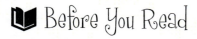 Before You Read

1. What are Wild Things?
2. How wild do you think the Wild Things are? Can you give some examples?
3. What type of book do you think this book will be? Funny? Scary? Why?
4. Why do you think the monster on the front cover is sleeping? Is he the Wild Thing?
5. Have you ever heard of other stories written by Maurice Sendak? If yes, which ones?

 As You Read

1. Why do you think Max's mom called him a "Wild Thing"?
2. Do you think it was a good idea for Max to answer back to his mom?
3. Have you ever been sent to bed without being able to eat your dinner? If yes, what did you do?
4. Did Max look upset for being sent to his room?
5. Why do you think his room was transformed?
6. What message do you think Max was trying to tell the Wild Things?
7. How different is Max from the beginning of the story and now at the middle? How do you think he will be at the end?
8. What's a rumpus? Have you ever made a rumpus? Where? When? With whom? Why?

Note to the Teacher: A rumpus is a very noisy commotion.

After You Read

1. Why do you think Max's supper was still hot? Do you think the supper was there for a long time?
2. What made his mom feed him supper?
3. Do you think he regrets being a Wild Thing?
4. Do you think he'll talk to his mom soon? What will he say?
5. What did you learn from this story?
6. If you were Max, what advice could you give other Wild Things?
7. Now as yourself, what advice could you give Max?

MAURICE SENDAK

Maurice Sendak was born in New York City on June 10, 1928. His parents had moved to the United States from Poland.

When he was very young, Maurice developed a wild imagination. He began to draw pictures from his imagination. Then, when he was a teenager, he fell in love with a movie which helped him decide to become an illustrator.

In 1947, his illustrations were first published in a science textbook. In 1951, he began his career as an illustrator for many children's books. His first major work was found in **A Hole Is to Dig** (1952), written by Ruth Kraus. He did many more projects with Kraus. Then he started writing and illustrating stories of his own.

Did You Know..?

• Maurice Sendak was inspired by Walt Disney's **Fantasia.**

• **Where the Wild Things Are** won the Caldecott Award in 1964.

• The "wild things" are based on his aunts and uncles who loved him so much!

10

Activity One

Circle the word or words that **rhyme** with the word in the

1.	broom	room	roam	ream	rame
2.	sneak	tooth	walk	talk	week
3.	vote	man	boat	map	mat
4.	wing	queen	bee	king	sea
5.	us	truck	duck	muck	rumpus

Activity Two

Read the word. **Say** the word. Which **vowel sound** does it have? **Circle** your answers.

1. claws

long a
short a
short e

2. day

long a
short a
silent a

3. best

short e
long e
silent e

4. eat

short e
long e
silent e

5. king

long i
short i
silent i

6. eyes

long i
silent i
short i

Aa Phonics

Activity Three

Fill in the blanks.

| wh | ch | th | sh |

1. a n o _ _ e r   2. m o _ _ e r   3. w i _ _ o u t

4. m i s _ _ i e f   5. _ _ o w e d   6. a n y _ _ i n g

7. _ _ i c h   8. _ _ e n   9. f i _ _

Activity Four

<u>Underline</u> the words that have a (short i) sound.

(Circle) the words that have a (long i) sound.

~~Cross~~ out the i if it is (silent.)

Examples: <u>in</u>   (wild)   sa~~i~~l

1. mischief   2. night   3. their

4. vines   5. I'll   6. king

7. kind   8. magic   9. terrible

10. eyes   11. still   12. private

13. trick   14. wild   15. thing

Activity Five

Write a word from the story that has double consonants or double vowels. The first two have been done for you.

1. a l l

2. r o o m

3. ste_____ed

4. sme_____ed

5. g_____d-bye

6. te_____ible

7. t_____th

8. ye_____ow

9. su_____er

10. sti_____

11. ro_____ed

12. r_____m

13. wa_____

14. w_____k

15. I'_____

Activity Six

Fill in the chart with the words from the list. Sound out the words carefully! Some words have Two vowel sounds. The first one has been done for you.

| trick | wall | yellow | claws | sail | blink |
| night | wave | eat | best | wild | teeth |

Long e
_____
_____

Long a
_____
_____

Long i
_____
_____

Short e
_____
_____

Short a
_____
_____

Short i
~~trick~~
_____

NAME: _____

Activity Seven

1. **Draw** a line from the beginning of the word to the end of the word. **Say** the word. **Write** the word on the line. The first one has been done for you.

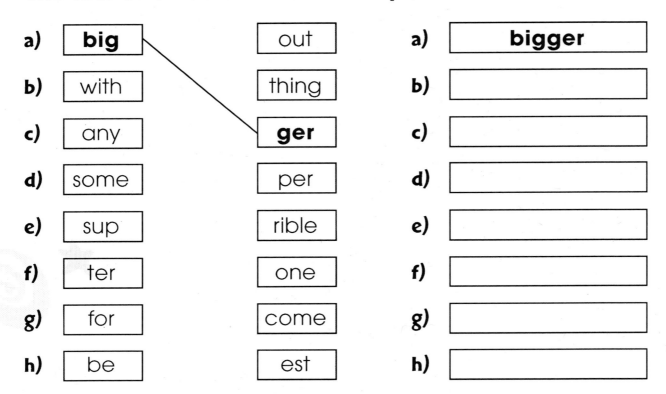

a)	**big**		out	**a)**	**bigger**	
b)	with		thing	**b)**		
c)	any		**ger**	**c)**		
d)	some		per	**d)**		
e)	sup		rible	**e)**		
f)	ter		one	**f)**		
g)	for		come	**g)**		
h)	be		est	**h)**		

2. Choose **two** words from the list above. Use each word in a full sentence. Remember to begin your sentence with a **capital letter** and end it with a **period.**

Sentence One

_____

Sentence Two

_____

Activity Eight

Find the words in the story. Fill in the blanks with the letters from the list. The first one has been done for you.

ea   ui   ei   ou   oa

1. s <u>a</u> i l

2. y ___ ___ r

3. o c ___ ___ n

4. t h ___ ___ r

5. p l ___ ___ s e

6. c ___ ___ l i n g

7. a r ___ ___ n d

8. s ___ ___ t

9. b ___ ___ t

Activity Nine

Read the word. **Say** the word. How many different **vowel sounds** does it have? The first one has been done for you.

1. boat ⇨ ①
2. private ⇨ ◯
3. gnashed ⇨ ◯
4. rolled ⇨ ◯
5. terrible ⇨ ◯
6. showed ⇨ ◯
7. rumpus ⇨ ◯
8. forest ⇨ ◯
9. anything ⇨ ◯
10. frightened ⇨ ◯
11. stepped ⇨ ◯
12. claws ⇨ ◯

Aa Phonics

Activity Ten

Here are words from the story. Change the first letter or last letter to make a (new) word.

Examples:

| yet | ⇨ | (m) e t | | hat | ⇨ | h a (d) |

1. sent ⇨ ( ) e n t
2. room ⇨ ( ) o o m
3. bed ⇨ b e ( )
4. vines ⇨ ( ) i n e s
5. claw ⇨ c l a ( )
6. wall ⇨ ( ) a l l
7. tame ⇨ ( ) a m e
8. year ⇨ ( ) e a r

Activity Eleven

Fill in each blank with the correct word from the story.

1. | suit / suite | Max was wearing his wolf _____.

2. | nite / night | That very _____ in Max's room grew a forest.

3. | Max / Mix | _____ was the King of the wild things.

4. | grow / grew | The vines and trees in his room just seemed to _____.

5. | super / supper | His mom sent him to his room without his _____.

6. | tooth / teeth | The wild things showed their _____.

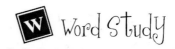

Activity One

Fill in each blank with the correct (verb) **from the story. Write each verb in the correct tense.**

1. The wild things _____ their terrible roars.

2. They _____ their terrible claws.

3. The wild things _____ their terrible teeth.

4. Max _____ good-bye.

5. He _____ good things to eat.

6. The ocean _____ by with a private boat.

Activity Two

These sentences are missing (punctuation.) **Put in the capital letters, period, and quotation marks where they belong.**

Example: and max said no ⟶ And Max said, "No!"

1. max stepped into his private boat

2. wild thing called out his mom

3. max said be still

4. max said I'll eat you up

5. and now cried max let the wild rumpus start

Activity Three

Here are words from the story in the **past** tense. Write each verb in the **present** tense.

1. was _____

2. hung _____

3. wore _____

4. came _____

5. made _____

6. found _____

7. sent _____

8. cried _____

9. grew _____

10. smelled _____

Activity Four

Write the words in proper sentence order.

1. terrible   They   teeth.   their   gnashed

_____

2. roared   roars?   their   Who   terrible

_____

3. Who   claws?   their   terrible   showed

_____

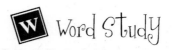

Activity Five

A full sentence is a complete thought. Are these sentences full sentences? Circle Yes or No.

1.	We love you so.	Yes	No
2.	Now stop!	Yes	No
3.	We'll eat you up.	Yes	No
4.	A forest grew.	Yes	No
5.	And now?	Yes	No
6.	That very night.	Yes	No

Activity Six

A pronoun is a word that is used instead of one name.
A pronoun is also used instead of a group of names.

Examples: it us

List all the pronouns you can find in the story.

_____

_____

_____

_____

_____

Activity Seven

A ⟨contraction⟩ is two words put together as one word, like this:

she will = she'll

In this example the word she'll is a contraction.

List all the contractions you can find in the story. Can you write down the two words that each contract is made of?

_____

_____

_____

Activity Eight

Write the words in ABC order.

1. king   trick   teeth   eyes   suit

_____

2. week   boat   nails   ceiling   room

_____

3. year   ocean   world   forest   night

_____

Activity Nine

1. The word **roar** is a verb found in the story. Find **ten** more verbs in the book. Write them in a list. Be sure to number your list!

Verbs

_____   _____

_____   _____

_____   _____

_____   _____

_____   _____

2. **Circle** your **two** favorite verbs in your list above. Use each verb in a full sentence of your own. Remember to begin each sentence with a capital letter and end it with a period.

Sentence One

_____

_____

Sentence Two

_____

_____

Activity Ten

1. A **noun** is a person, place or thing. Choose **four** nouns from the story. **Write** them on the lines. **Draw** a picture to show what the word means.

a) _____

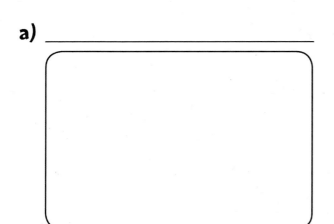

b) _____

c) _____

d) _____

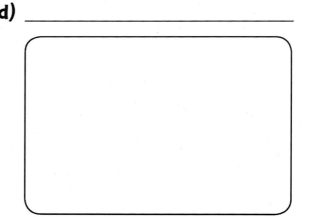

2. Choose **one** noun from Question 1 above. Use it in your own sentence. Write your sentence on the lines. Remember to begin your sentence with a **capital letter** and end it with a **period.**

_____

_____

Activity One

1. List (ten) words that describe Max. Remember to number your list.

MAX

_____   _____

_____   _____

_____   _____

_____   _____

_____   _____

2. <u>Underline</u> the words that tell what the monsters did in the story.

Roared their roar   gnashed their teeth

Rolled their eyes   showed their tails

3. (Circle) the words that describe where the story took place.

In Max's room   In Max's head

In Max's house   In Max's boat

NAME: _____

Activity Two

Fill in each blank with the correct word from the story.

sailed	yellow	place	world
magic	private	king	mischief
blinked	supper	hot	

1. Wearing his wolf suit, Max made _____ of one kind.

2. The walls of his bedroom became the _____ all around.

3. Max _____ off through night and day.

4. He came to a _____ where the wild things are.

5. He tamed them with a _____ trick.

6. Max was the _____ of the wild things.

7. His supper was _____ at the end of the story.

8. The wild things had _____ eyes and they were so frightened they never _____ .

9. Max sent the wild things off to bed without their _____ .

10. Max had his own _____ boat.

NAME: _____

Activity Three

Number the events from ❶ to ❿ in the order they happened in the story.

◯   Max smelled good things to eat so he gave up being king of where the wild things are.

◯   Max was sent to bed without having any supper.

◯   The wild things told Max not to go. They would eat him up because they loved him so.

◯   Max found his supper waiting for him, still hot.

◯   Max made mischief of one kind or another.

◯   Max was the king of the wild things.

◯   Max answered back to his mom.

◯   Together they had a wild rumpus.

◯   He was so mischievious, his mom called him, "WILD THING!"

◯   He took off in his private boat and landed at a place where the wild things were.

Comprehension

Activity Four

Circle T if the sentence is true.

Circle F if it is false (not true).

T	F	**1.**	Max had a hot supper.
T	F	**2.**	He flew to a place where the wild things were.
T	F	**3.**	Max could climb the vines until he reached the giant.
T	F	**4.**	Max was the king of the wild things.
T	F	**5.**	Just with a stare, he could tame them with the magic trick.
T	F	**6.**	They sailed off together through night and day.
T	F	**7.**	His mother joined them at the place where the wild things were.
T	F	**8.**	Max ran after the dog with a fork.
T	F	**9.**	He was proud to be the king of the wild things.
T	F	**10.**	Max felt lonely and he wanted to be loved.
T	F	**11.**	His father was also at the place where the wild things were.
T	F	**12.**	Among the wild things, Max saw his siblings and his friends from school.

NAME: _____

Activity Five

Put a check mark (✓) next to the answer that is correct.

1. **What type of day was Max having?**
   - ○ **A**   A good day
   - ○ **B**   A peaceful day
   - ○ **C**   A wild day

2. **Why did his mother send him to his room?**
   - ○ **A**   She was mean.
   - ○ **B**   Max was mean.
   - ○ **C**   The dog was mean.

3. **How long was Max gone?**
   - ○ **A**   Almost over a year
   - ○ **B**   Close to two years
   - ○ **C**   A few minutes

4. **How can you describe the roars, the teeth, the claws and the eyes of the wild things?**
   - ○ **A**   Funny
   - ○ **B**   Scary
   - ○ **C**   Terrible

5. **What did Max tell the wild things?**
   - ○ **A**   Calm down!
   - ○ **B**   Be still!
   - ○ **C**   Go to sleep!

© CLASSROOM COMPLETE PRESS

Where the Wild Things Are CC2104

NAME: _____

Activity Six

Complete each sentence with the word `before` or the word `after`. Write the word in the box.

	before	**after**

1. The forest grew in Max's room [   ] he was sent to his room without any supper.

2. The wild things gnashed their terrible teeth [   ] they roared their terrible roar.

3. Max found his supper waiting for him [   ] he took his long trip.

4. The wild things showed their terrible claws [   ] they rolled their terrible eyes.

5. Max waved good-bye [   ] he stepped into his private boat.

6. Max ran after the dog with a fork [   ] he ate his hot supper.

7. The wild rumpus started [   ] wild things begged Max to stay.

8. Max felt lonely [   ] sent the wild things to bed without their supper.

NAME: _____

Draw a picture of you making mischief.

Page One

Max made **mischief.** Then, his mom sent him to bed without any supper. Tell about a time when you made mischief. What happened? Were there any **consequences?**

Draw a picture of a time you felt mad about something.

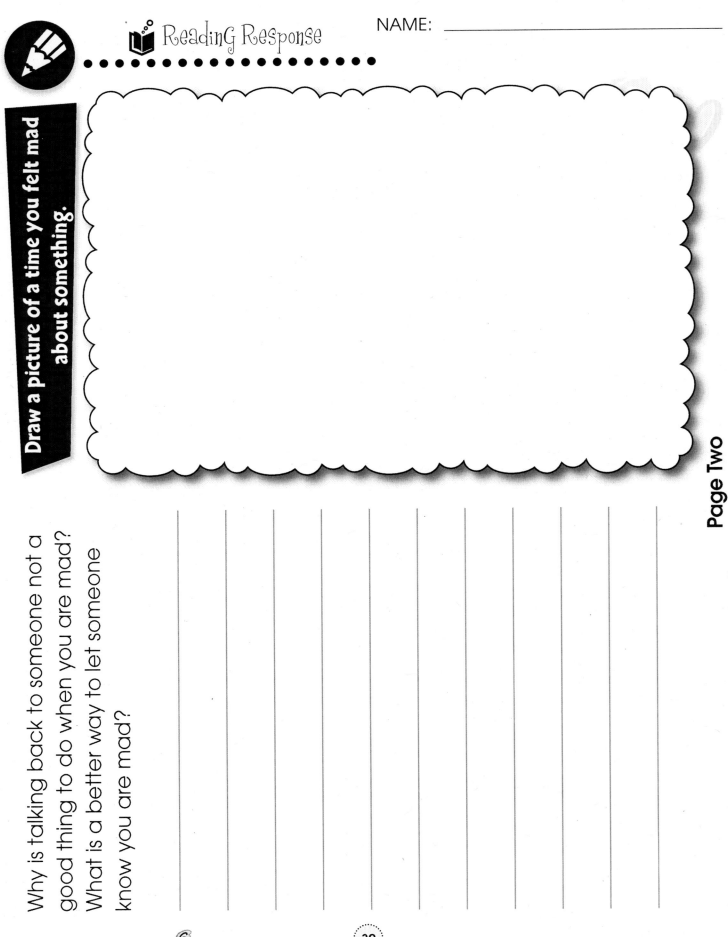

Page Two

Why is talking back to someone not a good thing to do when you are mad? What is a better way to let someone know you are mad?

NAME: _____

Draw a picture of you when you act mature.

Page Three

How can you show your feelings in a positive and mature way?

Where the Wild Things Are CC2104

Draw a picture of a creature or a place from your imagination.

Page Four

Max imagined being king of the wild things. What things do you imagine? Do you imagine monsters? Do you imagine that you go to far away places?

Draw a picture of Max's adventure.

Page Five

Max's meal was still hot after his adventure. How long do you think his adventure took?

_____
_____
_____
_____
_____
_____
_____
_____
_____
_____
_____

Draw a picture of an angry face.

Page Six

When you are angry, how do you deal with your feelings? Is it okay to be angry? Is it okay to show your anger? How is it okay and how is it not okay?

Activity One

Pretend that Max's mom has asked you for your expert advice on how to deal with her son. Write down six ideas on how to respond to her child when he misbehaves.

1 _____

_____

2 _____

_____

3 _____

_____

4 _____

_____

5 _____

_____

6 _____

_____

Activity Two

Write a letter to Max. In your letter give Max ideas on how he can control his anger. Let him know how you feel. Tell him he is not alone in his struggle to control his anger. Remember to include the date and your signature.

_____
(date)

Dear Max,

_____

_____

_____

_____

_____

_____

_____

_____

_____
(your signature)

Activity Three

Max's mom was nice to have left him a nice hot meal. Pretend that you are a wild thing. What supper would your mom leave for you? What meal would she make for you? What vegetables would you include? What about something to drink? Create a **Where the Wild Things Are Menu!** What do wild things eat?

Meal:

_____

_____

Vegetables:

_____

_____

Drink:

_____

_____

Dessert:

_____

_____

Activity Four

Look again at <u>Where the Wild Things Are.</u> Stop reading at the page where the wild things are having their wild rumpus. **Rewrite** the **ending** of the book. How will your ending be different from the author's? Will Max stay at the place of the wild things for life? Will he still be king? Will he meet a wild thing queen?

Activity Five

In the book, <u>Where The Wild Things Are</u>, Max was sent to his room by his mom. Max's dad isn't in the story at all. Rewrite the story from the dad's **point of view**. Tell why he's not in the story. Where was he? Why didn't he get to be in the book?

Activity Six

The author uses a lot of images in his book <u>Where the Wild Things Are</u> to help give the reader a feel for the story. One example is when Max runs after the dog with a fork. Rewrite the story using words that describe the illustrations. Imagine that you will read your story to someone who cannot see the book or the illustrations.

Crossword

Read the clues below. Write the answer where you find the correct number. Be careful! Some words go down. Some words go across.

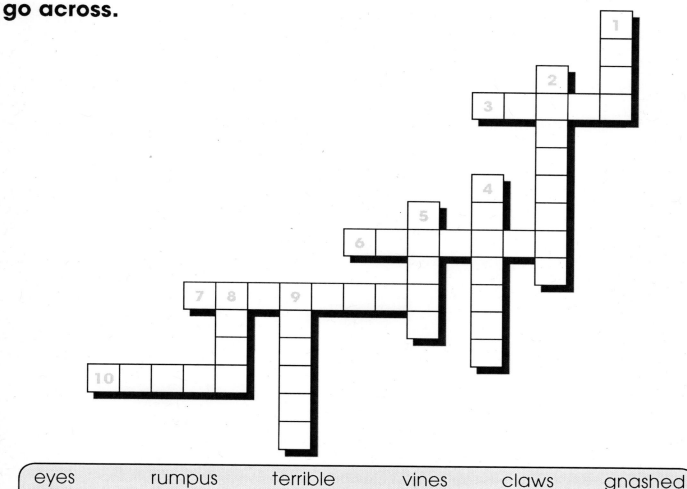

| eyes | rumpus | terrible | vines | claws | gnashed |
| private | week | mischief | blink | | |

Across

3. Close and open the eyes quickly
6. Max had a _____ boat.
7. The wild things had _____ teeth.
10. Sharp nails on an animal's toes

Down

1. Made up of seven days
2. Max made _____.
4. The wild things _____ their teeth.
5. Grapes grow on _____.
8. We see with our _____.
9. "Let the wild _____ start!" cried Max.

Word Search

1. Find the words in the Word Search puzzle. Circle them.

BOAT	FOREST	HUNG	KING
MAX	OCEAN	ROARED	SKY
STILL	TAMED	THING	WILD

E	J	C	R	V	R	J	F	D	K
M	X	A	M	O	U	B	O	E	I
E	Q	N	A	E	C	O	R	M	N
Y	Y	R	O	U	G	U	E	A	G
V	E	B	L	N	X	U	S	T	E
D	H	H	I	L	S	X	T	E	K
K	E	H	U	W	I	B	O	A	T
X	T	W	I	N	A	T	L	U	M
T	S	L	W	S	G	W	S	K	Y
B	D	G	C	M	Z	F	H	Y	U

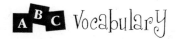

Vocabulary Cards

rumpus	claws
gnashed	vines
eyes	terrible
roared	ocean
blink	wild

Vocabulary Cards

mischief	**thing**
hung	**private**
tamed	**day**
still	**week**
almost	**year**

NAME: _____

Vocabulary Cards

NAME: _____

Comprehension Quiz

30

10

1. **Fill in the blanks.**

a) Max liked to wear his _____ suit.

b) His mom called him, "_____ _____!"

c) Max wasn't happy with his mom so he answered back,

"_____ _____ _____ _____!"

d) Max was sent to his room without _____.

e) Max had a wild imagination and he went to the place

where the _____ _____ are.

2. **Match the character with the item.**

4

Max's dog		a)	the king
Wolfsuit		b)	were really terrible
Max		c)	worn by a mischievous child
Wild things		d)	chased by Max with the fork

SUBTOTAL: /14

Where the Wild Things Are CC2104

Comprehension Quiz

Answer the questions in full sentences.

3. What does Max's dad say about Max's wild behavior?

_____

_____ ②

4. How did Max's mom react when he talked back to her?

_____

_____ ②

5. Why did Max feel like he was the king of the wild things?

_____

_____ ②

6. Why was his supper still hot?

_____

_____ ②

7. Where did Max go?

_____

_____ ②

8. How did Max get there?

_____

_____ ②

9. What grew and grew and grew?

_____

_____ ②

10. Why was Max so sad?

_____

_____ ②

SUBTOTAL: /16

1.
1. room
2. week
3. boat
4. king
5. rumpus

2.
1. short a 2. long a 3. short e
4. long e 5. short i 6. long i

3.
1. another 2. mother 3. without
4. mischief 5. showed 6. anything
7. which 8. then 9. fish

4.
1. mischief 2. night 3. their
4. vines 5. I'll 6. king
7. kind 8. magic 9. terrible
10. eyes 11. still 12. private
13. trick 14. wild 15. thing

5.
3. stepped
4. smelled 5. good-bye 6. terrible
7. teeth 8. yellow 9. supper
10. still 11. rolled 12. room
13. wall 14. week 15. I'll

6.

Long a:	Long i:
wave	night
sail	wild

Long e:	Short a:
teeth	wall
eat	claws

Short e:	short i:
yellow	trick
best	blink

7.
1.
b) without
c) anything
d) someone
e) supper
f) terrible
g) forest
h) become

2. Answers will vary

8.
2. year 3. ocean
4. their 5. please 6. ceiling
7. around 8. suit 9. boat

9.
2. 2 3. 1
4. 1 5. 3
6. 1 7. 2
8. 2 9. 3
10. 2 11. 1
12. 1

⑪ ⑫ ⑬ ⑭ ⑮

7.

we'll = we will

I'll = I will

don't = do not

8.

1. eyes, king, suit, teeth, trick

2. boat, ceiling, nails, room, week

3. forest, night, ocean, world, year

5.

1. Yes
2. Yes
3. Yes
4. Yes
5. No
6. No

6.

he

we

I

they

him

3.

1. is   2. hang
3. wear   4. come
5. make   6. find
7. send   8. cry
9. grow   10. smell

4.

1. They gnashed their terrible teeth.

2. Who roared their terrible roars?

3. Who showed their terrible claws?

1.

1. roared
2. showed
3. gnashed
4. waved
5. smelled
6. tumbled

2.

1. Max stepped into his private boat.

2. "Wild thing!" called out his mom.

3. Max said, "Be still!"

4. Max said, "I'll eat you up."

5. "And now," cried Max, "let the wild rumpus start!"

10.

Possible answers:

1. tent   2. boom
3. bet   4. lines
5. clap   6. tall
7. came   8. dear

11.

1. suit
2. night
3. Max
4. grow
5. supper
6. teeth

20

19

18

17

16

3. ⑨ ④ ⑧ ⑩ ① ⑥ ③ ⑦ ② ⑤

25

2.
1. mischief
2. world
3. sailed
4. place
5. magic
6. king
7. hot
8. yellow
   blinked
9. supper
10. private

24

1.
1. Answers will vary

2. All except showed their tails

3. All

23

1
1. Answers will vary

2. Answers will vary

22

9.
1. wore   came
    called   gnashed
    said   showed
    sent   rolled
    grew   tamed

2. Answers will vary

21

Down:

1. week
2. mischief
3. gnashed
5. vines
8. eyes
9. rumpus

Across:

3. blink
6. private
7. terrible
10. claws

29 30 31 32 33 34

Reading Response
All answers will vary

35 36 37 38 39 40

Writing Tasks
All answers will vary

6.

1. after

2. after

3. after

4. after

5. after

6. before

7. before

8. before

28

5.

1. Ⓒ C

2. Ⓑ B

3. Ⓒ C

4. Ⓒ C

5. Ⓑ B

27

4.

1. Ⓣ **2.** Ⓕ **3.** Ⓕ

4. Ⓣ **5.** Ⓣ

6. Ⓕ **7.** Ⓕ

8. Ⓣ **9.** Ⓣ **10.** Ⓣ **11.** Ⓕ

12. Ⓕ

26

© CLASSROOM COMPLETE PRESS

Where the Wild Things Are CC2104

41

Word Search Answers

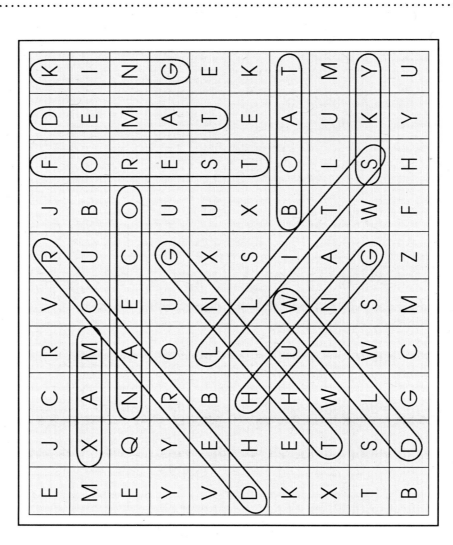

1.

a) wolf

b) Wild Thing

c) I'll eat you up!

d) supper

e) wild things

2.

a) Max

b) Wild things

c) Max's mom

d) Max's dog

3. Nothing – Max's dad isn't in the story.

4. Sent him to his room without any supper.

5. He told them what to do and he tamed them with a magic trick.

6. He was gone for a few minutes, not a year.

7. To the place where the wild things are

8. In his own private boat

9. The vines in Max's room

10. He wanted to be where someone would love him best of all.

Where the Wild Things Are CC2104

Dealing with Anger

HOW DO YOU DEAL WITH SITUATIONS THAT MAKE YOU ANGRY?

- In the first column of the chart write down things that make you angry. In the second column tell how you deal with your anger.
- In the third column think how you could have handled your anger in a more positive way.
- Share your answers with a partner.

SITUATION	HANDLED HOW	MORE POSITIVE WAY

Me and Max

· · · · · · · · · · · · · · · ·

DO YOU SEE YOURSELF IN MAX?

- In the first circle write words that descirbe you.
- In the second circle, write words that describe Max.
- Where the circles overlap, write words that describe both of you.

YOU

MAX

Sneaky Snake

FEED THE SNEAKY SNAKE!

- Write the **beginning** of the story in the snake's **head**.
- Continue the story in the snake's body.
- Write the ending of the story in the snake's **tail**.

Publication Listing
•••••••••••••••••
Ask Your Dealer About Our Complete Line

ENVIRONMENTAL STUDIES

ITEM #	TITLE
	MANAGING OUR WASTE SERIES
CC5764	Waste: At the Source
CC5765	Prevention, Recycling & Conservation
CC5766	Waste: The Global View
CC5767	Waste Management Big Book
	CLIMATE CHANGE SERIES
CC5769	Global Warming: Causes
CC5770	Global Warming: Effects
CC5771	Global Warming: Reduction
CC5772	Global Warming Big Book
	GLOBAL WATER SERIES
CC5773	Conservation: Fresh Water Resources
CC5774	Conservation: Ocean Water Resources
CC5775	Conservation: Waterway Habitats Resources
CC5776	Water Conservation Big Book
	CARBON FOOTPRINT SERIES
CC5778	Reducing Your Own Carbon Footprint
CC5779	Reducing Your School's Carbon Footprint
CC5780	Reducing Your Community's Carbon Footprint
CC5781	Carbon Footprint Big Book

LANGUAGE ARTS

ITEM #	TITLE
	WRITING SKILLS SERIES
CC1100	How to Write a Paragraph
CC1101	How to Write a Book Report
CC1102	How to Write an Essay
CC1103	Master Writing Big Book
	READING SKILLS SERIES
CC1116	Reading Comprehension
CC1117	Literary Devices
CC1118	Critical Thinking
CC1119	Master Reading Big Book

REGULAR & REMEDIAL EDUCATION
•••••••••••••••••
Reading Level 3-4 Grades 5-8

SCIENCE

ITEM #	TITLE
	ECOLOGY & THE ENVIRONMENT SERIES
CC4500	Ecosystems
CC4501	Classification & Adaptation
CC4502	Cells
CC4503	Ecology & The Environment Big Book
	MATTER & ENERGY SERIES
CC4504	Properties of Matter
CC4505	Atoms, Molecules & Elements
CC4506	Energy
CC4507	The Nature of Matter Big Book
	FORCE & MOTION SERIES
CC4508	Force
CC4509	Motion
CC4510	Simple Machines
CC4511	Force, Motion & Simple Machines Big Book
	SPACE & BEYOND SERIES
CC4512	Space - Solar Systems
CC4513	Space - Galaxies & The Universe
CC4514	Space - Travel & Technology
CC4515	Space Big Book
	HUMAN BODY SERIES
CC4516	Cells, Skeletal & Muscular Systems
CC4517	Nervous, Senses & Respiratory Systems
CC4518	Circulatory, Digestive & Reproductive Systems
CC4519	Human Body Big Book

SOCIAL STUDIES

ITEM #	TITLE
	NORTH AMERICAN GOVERNMENTS SERIES
CC5757	American Government
CC5758	Canadian Government
CC5759	Mexican Government
CC5760	Governments of North America Big Book
	WORLD GOVERNMENTS SERIES
CC5761	World Political Leaders
CC5762	World Electoral Processes
CC5763	Capitalism vs. Communism
CC5777	World Politics Big Book
	WORLD CONFLICT SERIES
CC5500	American Civil War
CC5511	American Revolutionary War
CC5512	American Wars Big Book
CC5501	World War I
CC5502	World War II
CC5503	World Wars I & II Big Book
CC5505	Korean War
CC5506	Vietnam War
CC5507	Korean & Vietnam Wars Big Book
CC5508	Persian Gulf War (1990-1991)
CC5509	Iraq War (2003-2010)
CC5510	Gulf Wars Big Book
	WORLD CONTINENTS SERIES
CC5750	North America
CC5751	South America
CC5768	The Americas Big Book
CC5752	Europe
CC5753	Africa
CC5754	Asia
CC5755	Australia
CC5756	Antarctica
	WORLD CONNECTIONS SERIES
CC5782	Culture, Society & Globalization
CC5783	Economy & Globalization
CC5784	Technology & Globalization
CC5785	Globalization Big Book
	MAPPING SKILLS SERIES
CC5786	Grades PK-2 Mapping Skills with Google Earth
CC5787	Grades 3-5 Mapping Skills with Google Earth
CC5788	Grades 6-8 Mapping Skills with Google Earth
CC5789	Grades PK-8 Mapping Skills with Google Earth Big Book

VISIT:

www.CLASSROOM COMPLETE PRESS.com

To view sample pages from each book

LITERATURE KITS™ (Novel Study Guides)

ITEM #	TITLE
	GRADES 1-2
CC2100	Curious George (H. A. Rey)
CC2101	Paper Bag Princess (Robert N. Munsch)
CC2102	Stone Soup (Marcia Brown)
CC2103	The Very Hungry Caterpillar (Eric Carle)
CC2104	Where the Wild Things Are (Maurice Sendak)
	GRADES 3-4
CC2300	Babe: The Gallant Pig (Dick King-Smith)
CC2301	Because of Winn-Dixie (Kate DiCamillo)
CC2302	The Tale of Despereaux (Kate DiCamillo)
CC2303	James and the Giant Peach (Roald Dahl)
CC2304	Ramona Quimby, Age 8 (Beverly Cleary)
CC2305	The Mouse and the Motorcycle (Beverly Cleary)
CC2306	Charlotte's Web (E.B. White)
CC2307	Owls in the Family (Farley Mowat)
CC2308	Sarah, Plain and Tall (Patricia MacLachlan)
CC2309	Matilda (Roald Dahl)
CC2310	Charlie & The Chocolate Factory (Roald Dahl)
CC2311	Frindle (Andrew Clements)
CC2312	M.C. Higgins, the Great (Virginia Hamilton)
CC2313	The Family Under The Bridge (N.S. Carlson)
	GRADES 5-6
CC2500	Black Beauty (Anna Sewell)
CC2501	Bridge to Terabithia (Katherine Paterson)
CC2502	Bud, Not Buddy (Christopher Paul Curtis)
CC2503	The Egypt Game (Zilpha Keatley Snyder)
CC2504	The Great Gilly Hopkins (Katherine Paterson)
CC2505	Holes (Louis Sachar)
CC2506	Number the Stars (Lois Lowry)
CC2507	The Sign of the Beaver (E.G. Speare)
CC2508	The Whipping Boy (Sid Fleischman)
CC2509	Island of the Blue Dolphins (Scott O'Dell)
CC2510	Underground to Canada (Barbara Smucker)
CC2511	Loser (Jerry Spinelli)
CC2512	The Higher Power of Lucky (Susan Patron)
CC2513	Kira-Kira (Cynthia Kadohata)
CC2514	Dear Mr. Henshaw (Beverly Cleary)
CC2515	The Summer of the Swans (Betsy Byars)
CC2516	Shiloh (Phyllis Reynolds Naylor)
CC2517	A Single Shard (Linda Sue Park)
CC2518	Hoot (Carl Hiaasen)
CC2519	Hatchet (Gary Paulsen)
CC2520	The Giver (Lois Lowry)
CC2521	The Graveyard Book (Neil Gaiman)
CC2522	The View From Saturday (E.L. Konigsburg)
CC2523	Hattie Big Sky (Kirby Larson)
CC2524	When You Reach Me (Rebecca Stead)
CC2525	Criss Cross (Lynne Rae Perkins)
CC2526	A Year Down Yonder (Richard Peck)
	GRADES 7-8
CC2700	Cheaper by the Dozen (Frank B. Gilbreth)
CC2701	The Miracle Worker (William Gibson)
CC2702	The Red Pony (John Steinbeck)
CC2703	Treasure Island (Robert Louis Stevenson)
CC2704	Romeo & Juliet (William Shakespeare)
CC2705	Crispin: The Cross of Lead (Avi)
	GRADES 9-12
CC2001	To Kill A Mockingbird (Harper Lee)
CC2002	Angela's Ashes (Frank McCourt)
CC2003	The Grapes of Wrath (John Steinbeck)
CC2004	The Good Earth (Pearl S. Buck)
CC2005	The Road (Cormac McCarthy)
CC2006	The Old Man and the Sea (Ernest Hemingway)

REGULAR EDUCATION

LANGUAGE ARTS

ITEM #	TITLE
	READING RESPONSE FORMS SERIES
CC1106	Reading Response Forms: Grades 1-2
CC1107	Reading Response Forms: Grades 3-4
CC1108	Reading Response Forms: Grades 5-6
CC1109	Reading Response Forms Big Book: Grades 1-6
	WORD FAMILIES SERIES
CC1110	Word Families - Short Vowels: Grades PK-1
CC1111	Word Families - Long Vowels: Grades PK-1
CC1112	Word Families - Vowels Big Book: Grades K-1
	SIGHT & PICTURE WORDS SERIES
CC1113	High Frequency Sight Words: Grades PK-1
CC1114	High Frequency Picture Words: Grades PK-1
CC1115	Sight & Picture Words Big Book Grades PK-1

INTERACTIVE WHITEBOARD SOFTWARE

ITEM #	TITLE
	WORD FAMILIES SERIES
CC7112	Word Families - Short Vowels Grades PK-2
CC7113	Word Families - Long Vowels Grades PK-2
CC7114	Word Families - Vowels Big Box Grades PK-2
	SIGHT & PICTURE WORDS SERIES
CC7100	High Frequency Sight Words Grades PK-2
CC7101	High Frequency Picture Words Grades PK-2
CC7102	Sight & Picture Words Big Box Grades PK-2
	WRITING SKILLS SERIES
CC7104	How to Write a Paragraph Grades 3-8
CC7105	How to Write a Book Report Grades 3-8
CC7106	How to Write an Essay Grades 3-8
CC7107	Master Writing Big Box Grades 3-8
	READING SKILLS SERIES
CC7108	Reading Comprehension Grades 3-8
CC7109	Literary Devices Grades 3-8
CC7110	Critical Thinking Grades 3-8
CC7111	Master Reading Big Box Grades 3-8
	PRINCIPLES & STANDARDS OF MATH SERIES
CC7315	Five Strands of Math Big Box Grades PK-2
CC7316	Five Strands of Math Big Box Grades 3-5
CC7317	Five Strands of Math Big Box Grades 6-8
	SPACE & BEYOND SERIES
CC7557	Solar System Grades 3-8
CC7558	Galaxies & The Universe Grades 3-8
CC7559	Space Travel & Technology Grades 3-8
CC7560	Space Big Box Grades 3-8
	HUMAN BODY SERIES
CC7549	Cells, Skeletal & Muscular Systems Grades 3-8
CC7550	Senses, Nervous & Respiratory Systems Grades 3-8
CC7551	Circulatory, Digestive & Reproductive Systems Grades 3-8
CC7552	Human Body Big Box Grades 3-8
	FORCE, MOTION & SIMPLE MACHINES SERIES
CC7553	Force Grades 3-8
CC7554	Motion Grades 3-8
CC7555	Simple Machines Grades 3-8
CC7556	Force, Motion & Simple Machines Big Box Grades 3-8
	CLIMATE CHANGE SERIES
CC7747	Global Warming: Causes Grades 3-8
CC7748	Global Warming: Effects Grades 3-8
CC7749	Global Warming: Reduction Grades 3-8
CC7750	Global Warming Big Box Grades 3-8

MATHEMATICS

ITEM #	TITLE
	PRINCIPLES & STANDARDS OF MATH SERIES
CC3100	Grades PK-2 Number & Operations Task Sheets
CC3101	Grades PK-2 Algebra Task Sheets
CC3102	Grades PK-2 Geometry Task Sheets
CC3103	Grades PK-2 Measurement Task Sheets
CC3104	Grades PK-2 Data Analysis & Probability Task Sheets
CC3105	Grades PK-2 Five Strands of Math Big Book Task Sheets
CC3106	Grades 3-5 Number & Operations Task Sheets
CC3107	Grades 3-5 Algebra Task Sheets
CC3108	Grades 3-5 Geometry Task Sheets
CC3109	Grades 3-5 Measurement Task Sheets
CC3110	Grades 3-5 Data Analysis & Probability Task Sheets
CC3111	Grades 3-5 Five Strands of Math Big Book Task Sheets
CC3112	Grades 6-8 Number & Operations Task Sheets
CC3113	Grades 6-8 Algebra Task Sheets
CC3114	Grades 6-8 Geometry Task Sheets
CC3115	Grades 6-8 Measurement Task Sheets
CC3116	Grades 6-8 Data Analysis & Probability Task Sheets
CC3117	Grades 6-8 Five Strands of Math Big Book Task Sheets
	PRINCIPLES & STANDARDS OF MATH SERIES
CC3200	Grades PK-2 Number & Operations Drill Sheets
CC3201	Grades PK-2 Algebra Drill Sheets
CC3202	Grades PK-2 Geometry Drill Sheets
CC3203	Grades PK-2 Measurement Drill Sheets
CC3204	Grades PK-2 Data Analysis & Probability Drill Sheets
CC3205	Grades PK-2 Five Strands of Math Big Book Drill Sheets
CC3206	Grades 3-5 Number & Operations Drill Sheets
CC3207	Grades 3-5 Algebra Drill Sheets
CC3208	Grades 3-5 Geometry Drill Sheets
CC3209	Grades 3-5 Measurement Drill Sheets
CC3210	Grades 3-5 Data Analysis & Probability Drill Sheets
CC3211	Grades 3-5 Five Strands of Math Big Book Drill Sheets
CC3212	Grades 6-8 Number & Operations Drill Sheets
CC3213	Grades 6-8 Algebra Drill Sheets
CC3214	Grades 6-8 Geometry Drill Sheets
CC3215	Grades 6-8 Measurement Drill Sheets
CC3216	Grades 6-8 Data Analysis & Probability Drill Sheets
CC3217	Grades 6-8 Five Strands of Math Big Book Drill Sheets
	PRINCIPLES & STANDARDS OF MATH SERIES
CC3300	Grades PK-2 Number & Operations Task & Drill Sheets
CC3301	Grades PK-2 Algebra Task & Drill Sheets
CC3302	Grades PK-2 Geometry Task & Drill Sheets
CC3303	Grades PK-2 Measurement Task & Drill Sheets
CC3304	Grades PK-2 Data Analysis & Probability Task & Drill
CC3306	Grades 3-5 Number & Operations Task & Drill Sheets
CC3307	Grades 3-5 Algebra Task & Drill Sheets
CC3308	Grades 3-5 Geometry Task & Drill Sheets
CC3309	Grades 3-5 Measurement Task & Drill Sheets
CC3310	Grades 3-5 Data Analysis & Probability Task & Drill
CC3312	Grades 6-8 Number & Operations Task & Drill Sheets
CC3313	Grades 6-8 Algebra Task & Drill Sheets
CC3314	Grades 6-8 Geometry Task & Drill Sheets
CC3315	Grades 6-8 Measurement Task & Drill Sheets
CC3316	Grades 6-8 Data Analysis & Probability Task & Drill